SUSIE BROOKS

LET'S MAKE ART

WITH

EVERYDAY THINGS

Published in paperback in Great Britain in 2019 by Wayland

Printed in China

Wayland
An imprint of
Hachette Children's Group
Part of Hodder and Stoughton
Carmelite House
50 Victoria Embankment
London EC4Y 0DZ

An Hachette UK Company
www.hachette.co.uk
www.hachettechildrens.co.uk

Editor: Elizabeth Brent
Design: nicandlou

CONTENTS

Forky Fun p.6-7

Key Cartoons p.16-17

Lolly-stick Puppets p.24-25

LET'S MAKE ART!

LOOK ALL AROUND YOU, INDOORS AND OUTDOORS — WHAT CAN YOU FIND TO MAKE INTO ART? THIS BOOK IS PACKED WITH EXCITING IDEAS TO HELP YOU TURN ORDINARY THINGS INTO EXTRAORDINARY THINGS!

WHAT YOU NEED

Search at home for things that you can print with, paint on, cut out or draw around. In this book we'll make art using coins, keys, kitchen paper, cling film, toilet rolls, lolly sticks, sponges, forks, cheese graters, freezer-bag ties and even salt and soap! Check your recycling for old newspaper, envelopes and cereal packets and save them for your work too.

FOR THE PROJECTS IN THIS BOOK IT ALSO HELPS TO HAVE A FEW BASIC ART SUPPLIES:

- ✓ a pencil and rubber
- ✓ ready-mix paints
- ✓ paintbrushes
- ✓ paper plates or a paint palette
- ✓ coloured ink pads
- ✓ felt-tip pens
- ✓ crayons or oil pastels
- ✓ scissors
- ✓ glue
- ✓ plain white paper or card
- ✓ coloured paper or card, including black
- ✓ string, thread or wool
- ✓ a hole punch
- ✓ newspaper

HANDY HINTS

Before you start, lay down plenty of newspaper to protect the surface you're working on.

Painted paper will dry more quickly if you leave it in a warm place like an airing cupboard or by a radiator.

Sometimes painted paper wrinkles as it dries. Don't worry - you can flatten it later under a pile of books.

Always wait for your paint to dry before drawing or sticking on details.

Nail scissors are handy for cutting small paper shapes. Some craft scissors have a special zigzag blade for fancy edges.

If you don't have paper in the colour you want, you can always paint your own.

When you see this LOGO, you might want to ask an adult to help.

There are templates on pages 30-31 to help you draw some useful shapes, but don't try to copy everything exactly. Half the fun of art is using your imagination and testing ideas of your own!

FORKY FUN

PRINT THESE FUN ANIMALS WITH AN EVERYDAY FORK — BUT REMEMBER TO WASH THE PAINT OFF AFTERWARDS!

 Spread some paint on to a paper plate and dip in the back of a fork. Practise making prong prints, like below, on to white paper.

ONE FORK

THREE FORK PRINTS IN A ROW

 To make a cat, print a round head like this. For the body, make several rows of prints underneath each other.

LOTS OF FORK PRINTS IN A CIRCLE — TURN THE PAPER AS YOU GO

PAINT ON SOME EARS AND A TAIL USING A PAINTBRUSH.

ADD SOME WHISKERS.

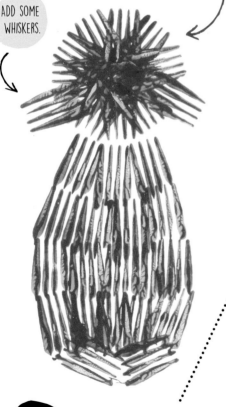

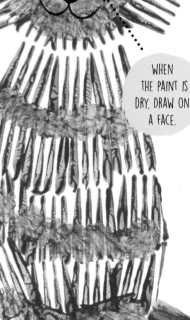

WHEN THE PAINT IS DRY, DRAW ON A FACE.

3 While the paint is still wet, scrunch up a piece of kitchen paper and use it to blot the paint in the middle of the head. Add some stripes to the body, too.

What other animals
can you print?

TRY A WHITE SHEEP ...

USE COLOURED
PAPER. WHY NOT
FORK-PRINT SOME
GREEN GRASS.

OR A HEDGEHOG ...

OR 'FORKUPINE'!
PRINT THE FORKY
PRICKLES FIRST,
THEN PAINT ON
A HEAD.

OR SOME FORK FLOWERS!

PRESS THE FORK
DOWN AND ROCK IT
BACKWARDS TO PRINT
THE PART BELOW THE
PRONGS. THEN PAINT
ON A STALK AND
LEAVES, AND YOU
HAVE A FLOWER!

BRILLIANT BALLOONS

USE SCRAPS OF OLD FABRIC, FELT OR KITCHEN CLOTHS TO MAKE THIS HOT-AIR-BALLOON COLLAGE!

1 Start by making a balloon template. Fold a piece of paper, about A5 size, in half. Draw a shape like this by the folded edge.

CUT OUT THE SHAPE AND OPEN IT OUT LIKE THIS TO MAKE A TEMPLATE.

2 Cut several strips of fabric, a bit longer than the template's width. Glue them in stripes on to another piece of paper, until you have a block that's as tall as the template.

3 Draw around your template on to the fabric block and cut out the balloon shape. Glue it on to a piece of white paper.

4 Now make the basket. Cut a shape from fabric and glue it about 2 cm below the balloon. Stick two pieces of thread or wool between the two.

FINGERPRINT A PERSON TO GO IN THE BASKET.

8

WHY NOT MAKE A COLLECTION OF BALLOONS?

CUT SQUARE PIECES OF FABRIC AND ARRANGE THEM IN A BLOCK. STICK THEM ON TO PAPER BEFORE CUTTING OUT THE BALLOON, AS YOU DID IN STEP 2.

YOU CAN CUT FANCY EDGES WITH ZIGZAG CRAFT SCISSORS.

ADD A FACE, HAIR AND SOME WAVING ARMS TO YOUR PERSON!

tip

Thumbprint some birds then draw on beaks, wings and tails. You could stick fabric clouds above them and draw lines to make them look as if they're dangling!

THIS BUSH WAS CUT FROM AN OLD SOCK.

9

ICE-CREAM BUNTING

RECYCLE CARD PACKAGING INTO A DELICIOUS DECORATION! OLD CEREAL PACKETS WORK WELL FOR THIS PROJECT.

1 Draw a diamond shape on a piece of white card, as shown. If your card is not white, glue some white paper over it. You'll need at least five or six of these shapes.

THERE ARE TEMPLATES FOR SOME OF THE SHAPES ON P.30.

2 Cut out the shapes and use a hole punch to make two holes in the top part, like this.

FOR AN ICE LOLLY, CUT OUT A LONG CARD LOLLY STICK, THEN PUNCH A HOLE IN THE TOP OF IT. THREAD THE WOOL THROUGH, THEN GLUE A STRIPY LOLLY SHAPE ON TOP.

WHY NOT MAKE A CHOCOLATE FLAKE OR A CHERRY?

3 Mix some yellow paint with a little flour or white glue to thicken it. Use this to paint the cones. While the paint is wet, scratch patterns into it using the end of your brush.

4 Cut out some ice-cream shapes from white card – one for each cone. Paint them with thickened paint, as in Step 3. Swirl patterns into the paint. You could scatter on glitter or even real sugar sprinkles to decorate!

tip

The paint will take several hours to dry. Be patient! You could try another project while you wait.

5 When the paint is dry, thread your cones on to a long piece of wool or string. Space them out and glue an ice-cream shape over each cone.

Your bunting is ready to hang!

TRY USING NAIL POLISH FOR A DRIZZLE OF SAUCE.

KITCHEN CROCS

PAINT KITCHEN PAPER TO MAKE THIS SUPER—SCALY CROCODILE COLLAGE!

1 Lay a sheet of kitchen paper on some newspaper. Use thin, watery paint to colour the kitchen paper green and yellow. Leave it to dry.

The colours will run into each other!

2 When the paper is dry, cut out or tear shapes like these for a crocodile.

3 Glue the shapes on to a piece of white paper. Paint on two white eyes with black dots in the middle. You could tear some small strips from the leftover green kitchen paper and glue them to the tail to make stripes.

TRY PAINTING SOME MORE SHEETS OF KITCHEN PAPER IN DIFFERENT COLOURS. WHEN THEY'RE DRY, TEAR STRIPS OF BLUE FOR A LAKE, AND STICK THEM NEAR YOUR CROCODILE'S FEET.

ADD SOME PAPER CLAWS IF YOU LIKE.

WHY NOT ADD A SWIMMING CROC IN THE LAKE?

YOU COULD CUT OUT AND STICK ON SOME BIRDS, REEDS AND LILIES. THERE ARE SOME TEMPLATES ON P.31 IF YOU NEED THEM.

SOAPY SOLAR SYSTEM

MIX WATERY PAINT WITH SOAP AND SALT, TO MAKE A PICTURE THAT'S OUT OF THIS WORLD!

1 Rub a bar of soap back and forth over a piece of white card or paper. Brush watery paint over the top and leave it to dry. You'll get a streaky effect like this.

3 When the paint is dry, draw around a cup and cut out circles for planets.

CUT A STRIP LIKE THIS AND STICK IT ACROSS A PLANET FOR A RING.

YOU COULD USE ZIGZAG CRAFT SCISSORS TO MAKE A FIERY SUN OR STARS.

2 For a speckled effect, sprinkle salt over the wet paint and brush it off when dry.

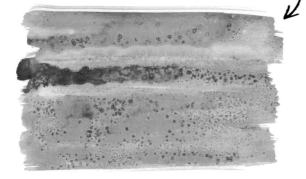

tip
While the paint is drying, repeat Step 1 in a few different colours and paint the background for Step 4.

14

4 For your spacey background, swirl the bar of soap in a spiral over a large sheet of white card or paper. Brush watery dark blue paint all over it and let it dry.

GLUE ON YOUR PLANETS, STARS AND SUN. YOU COULD ADD AN ALIEN OR A SHOOTING STAR!

KEY CARTOONS

USE KEYS TO MAKE THESE PRINTS, THEN TURN
THEM INTO QUIRKY CARTOON CHARACTERS.

1 Ask an adult for a spare key that you can use. Press it on to a coloured ink pad, then print it on white paper.

2 For a dog, draw a circle with a loop on top, like this.

3 Try making two key prints with the narrow ends together.

THEY COULD BECOME A FACE ...

There are templates on p.30 if you need them.

SCRIBBLE THE EARS AND NECK, AND DRAW IN EYES AND A SMILEY MOUTH.

... OR AN OWL!

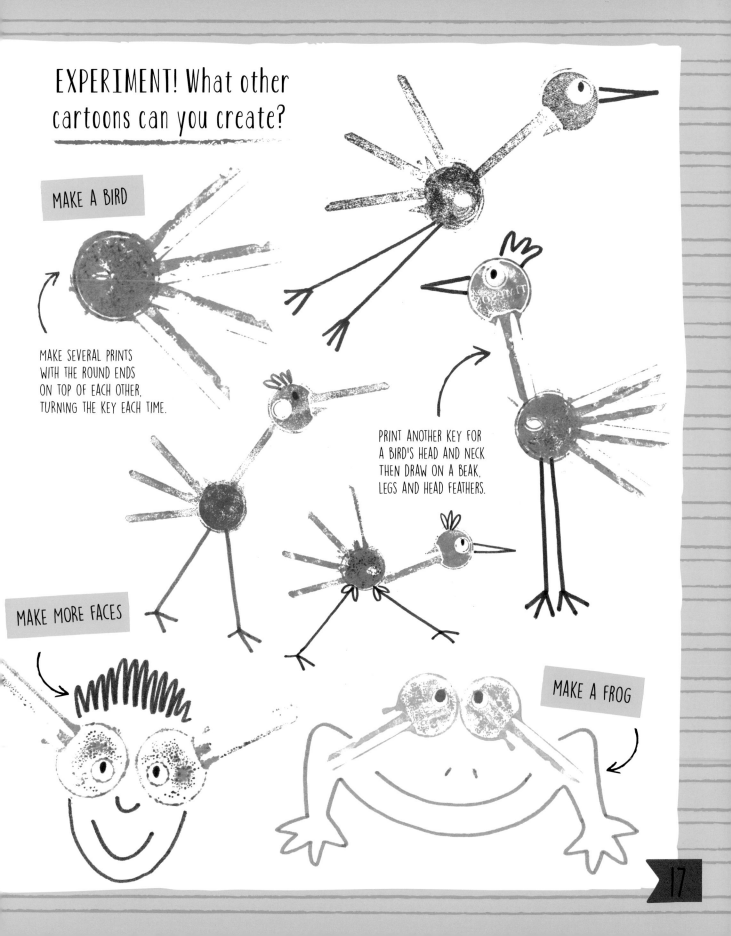

EXPERIMENT! What other cartoons can you create?

MAKE A BIRD

MAKE SEVERAL PRINTS WITH THE ROUND ENDS ON TOP OF EACH OTHER, TURNING THE KEY EACH TIME.

PRINT ANOTHER KEY FOR A BIRD'S HEAD AND NECK THEN DRAW ON A BEAK, LEGS AND HEAD FEATHERS.

MAKE MORE FACES

MAKE A FROG

17

TEXTURED TURTLES

MAKE AN UNDERWATER WORLD BY PRINTING FROM A PIECE OF CLING FILM!

1 Tear off some cling film at least the size of a piece of A4 paper. Lay it over newspaper, then use a damp sponge to cover it with blue paint. Press a piece of white A4 paper on top, then peel the paper off.

2 While the paper is drying, make a couple more cling-film prints using yellow and green paper. When they are dry, cut out shapes for a turtle – there are templates on p.31.

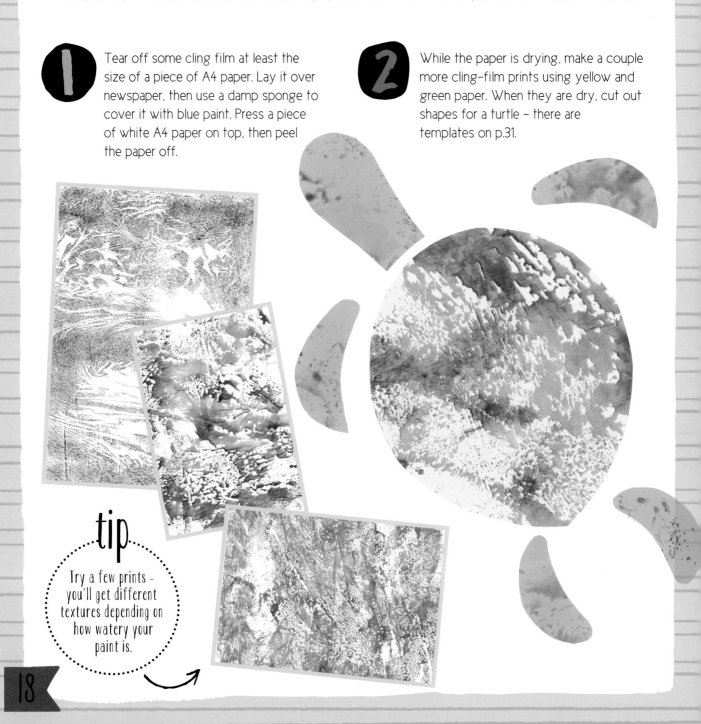

tip

Try a few prints – you'll get different textures depending on how watery your paint is.

3 Stick the turtle on to the blue background. You could cut out some oval shapes in a different colour and stick them on the shell, too.

CLING—FILM PRINT SOME DIFFERENT COLOURED PAPER TO MAKE ROCKS AND STARFISH!

MONEY TREES

USE A CLUSTER OF COIN RUBBINGS TO MAKE SOME MAGICAL MONEY TREES!

1 Try to use a mixture of different coins. Lay a piece of thin paper over a coin, and rub a wax crayon on the surface.

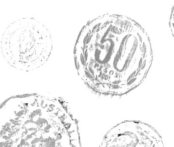

2 For a brighter effect, brush watery paint over your rubbing. The crayon will resist the paint! Don't worry about neat edges – you're going to cut the coins out.

tip
Hold the paper over the coin with one finger, to keep it steady as you work.

3 Make lots of colourful rubbings and cut them out. Keep them safe while you paint a white tree trunk and branches on to coloured paper or card. You could scratch lines into the trunk using the end of your brush, to look like bark. Let it dry.

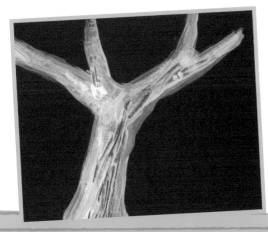

4 Now glue your paper coins on to your tree, like leaves.

Here are some other ideas you can try ...

LUCKY BOUQUET

Cut strips of green paper for stalks and glue them down. Glue on a piece of doily, then stick a cluster of coins on top. Add two paper triangles and a square for the bow.

TREE IN A TUB

Stick down a cluster of coins. Glue on a trunk shape cut from coloured paper, and a piece of cupcake case for a pot.

STICK ALL THE COIN RUBBINGS ON TO COLOURED PAPER OR CARD.

CHRISTMAS TREE

Cut out a green paper triangle and a yellow trunk. Glue on pieces of doily for decoration, and stick the coins on top.

YOU COULD FOLD THE PAPER FIRST, TO MAKE A GREETINGS CARD WITH A LUCKY COIN TREE ON THE FRONT.

SPONGY SNOWMEN

USE A SPONGE AND A CARDBOARD STENCIL TO PAINT A FLURRY OF SNOWMAN FRIENDS.

1 To make the stencil, draw two circles like this on to thin cardboard. You can use cups or rolls of tape as a guide. Cut out the shape, <u>keeping the outside piece whole.</u>

2 Now lay the stencil on a larger piece of cardboard. Dip a sponge in thick white paint and dab it all over the cut-out shape.

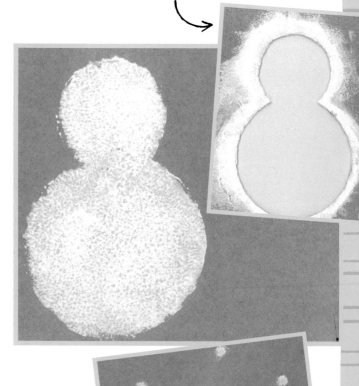

tip
If you keep the inside piece too, you can use it for the puppet on p.24!

3 Use the sponge to paint a line of snow at the bottom. Tear off a small piece of sponge to paint some snowflakes.

4 Cut a strip of sponge and cover one edge in black paint. Press it down to print two arms. Print the eyes and buttons with the end of a pencil, and paint a line of dots for the mouth.

5 Now dress up your snowman! Use your sponge to dab coloured paint on to paper.

TRY A CLOWN HAT, BOW TIE OR SOME SUNGLASSES!

CUT OUT A TRIANGULAR NOSE FROM ORANGE CARD OR PACKAGING AND STICK IT ON.

CUT OUT HAT AND SCARF SHAPES TO STICK ON.

HAT

SCARF

LOLLY-STICK PUPPETS

THESE PUPPETS ARE A GREAT WAY TO RECYCLE OLD FOOD PACKAGING AND LOLLY STICKS.

1 Draw two circles like this on a piece of thin cardboard, as you did for the snowman on p.22. Cut out the whole shape.

2 Cut a circle of white paper, the same size as the big circle, and paint or stick on red stripes. Glue this on to your cardboard shape.

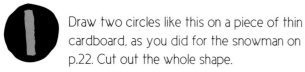

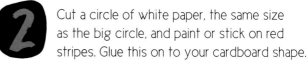

There are templates on p.31 if you need them.

3 Paint or stick on a beard shape. This one was cut from a magazine. Draw on a face with an eyepatch.

4 Cut out a black pirate's hat and paint on white crossbones. Cut out a card hand, hook and boot. Stick each one to a wire freezer-bag tie or pipe cleaner – tape them in place at the back.

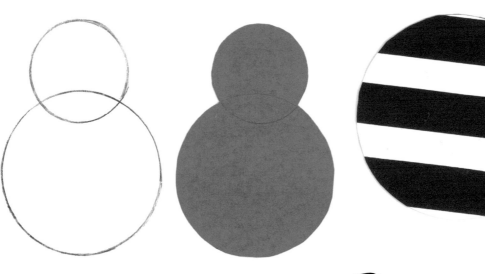

HOOK

HAND

PIRATE HAT

BOOT

Tape the other end of each arm and leg to the back of the pirate's body. Glue the hat on to the head. You could stick on a sword cut from foil packaging.

What other puppet characters can you make?

 TAPE ON A LOLLY STICK FOR A HANDLE THAT DOUBLES AS A WOODEN LEG!

TRY AN ASTRONAUT

Stick two circles of newspaper on to another cardboard base as before. Decorate with shapes cut from coloured paper and foil.

Make a thumbprint on a small circle of white paper. Draw on a face and stick it on the astronaut's head.

FLOWERS AND FIREWORKS

CREATE SOME BRIGHT SPARKS WITH THE CARDBOARD TUBE FROM THE MIDDLE OF A TOILET ROLL!

PROJECT

1. Start by cutting slits up from one end of the tube. The slits should be about 4 cm long and roughly 1 cm apart.

SPLAY OUT THE SPLIT ENDS, LIKE THIS.

2. Squeeze some red and yellow paint on to a paper plate. Dip the splayed end of the tube into it and move it around until the strips are all coated. Press the tube on to paper, and you'll get a shape like this.

3. You could turn your pattern into a flower or a sun. Use your fingertip to print dots in the middle. Paint in a stalk and leaves, or cut them from green paper and glue them on.

PROJECT
2

For a firework display, add some white paint to your plate and print on black paper. Dip the splayed ends of the tube back into the paint for each firework.

SPONGE SOME RED AND YELLOW PAINT OVER THEM SO THEY GLOW!

YOU COULD CUT OUT SOME BUILDING SHAPES FROM NEWSPAPER AND GLUE THEM BELOW THE FIREWORKS.

PATCHWORK PATTERNS

YOU CAN MAKE RUBBINGS FROM ALL SORTS OF EVERYDAY ITEMS AND TURN THEM INTO BEAUTIFUL DESIGNS.

1 Find a few things that have an interesting texture on their surface – the examples on this page will give you some ideas. Lay a piece of thin paper over each one and rub with a crayon or oil pastel.

THESE PATTERNS CAME FROM THE DIFFERENT SIDES OF A CHEESE GRATER.

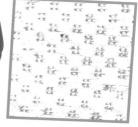

FOR STRIPES TRY:

CORRUGATED CARD

A GRIDDLE PAN

A SLOTTED SPATULA

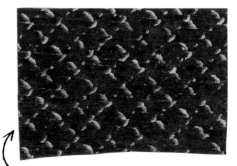

TRY RUBBING GENTLY ON COLOURED TISSUE PAPER

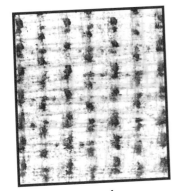

A MESH BAG

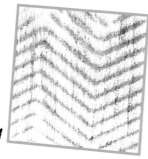

THE BOTTOM OF A SHOE

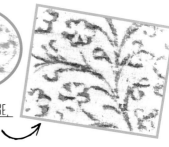

PATTERNS ON CARVED FURNITURE, BELT BUCKLES OR TRINKETS

2 Make a selection of rubbings, then cut out squares, rectangles, circles and triangles from them. Arrange them in patterns and glue them on to scrap paper or card.

TRY MAKING A POSTCARD!

CUT STRIPS OF A SIMILAR WIDTH AND ARRANGE THEM AROUND A PICTURE, LIKE A FRAME!

SMALLER SHAPES MAKE GREAT GIFT TAGS OR BOOKMARKS.

YOU COULD TAPE A COCKTAIL STICK OR SKEWER TO THE BACK, FOR A FUN FLAG DECORATION.

TEMPLATES

KEY CARTOONS
P.16–17

ICE–CREAM
BUNTING
P.10–11

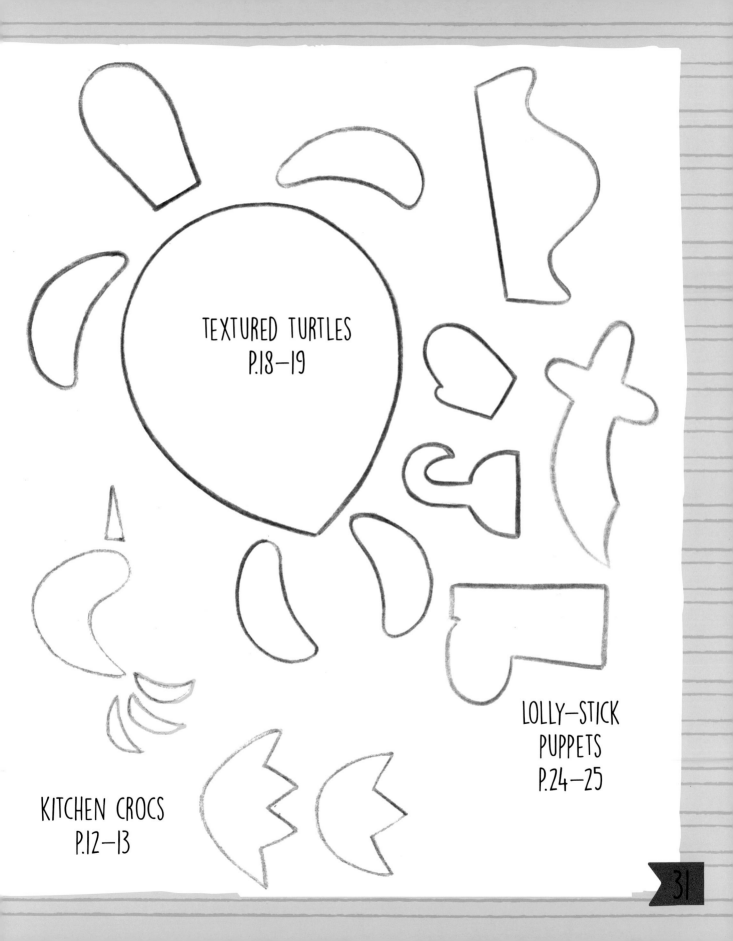

TEXTURED TURTLES
P.18—19

LOLLY—STICK
PUPPETS
P.24—25

KITCHEN CROCS
P.12—13

GLOSSARY

COLLAGE art made by sticking bits of paper, fabric or other materials on to a surface

CORRUGATED ridged, like the inside layer of some cardboard

PRINT to make an image by pressing a painted or inked object on to paper, card or another surface. The printed image comes out in reverse.

SPLAYED spread out and apart

STENCIL a thin piece of cardboard (or other material) with a shape cut out of it. A design can be made by placing the stencil on paper and applying paint or ink through the hole.

TEMPLATE a shape used as a guideline to draw or cut around

TEXTURE the feel or appearance of a surface. Rough or raised textures, such as the sides of a cheese grater, can be used as a base to make rubbings.